CRYSTAL ENERGY

Monnica Hackl has many years experience in Chinese and Shamanic healing, and is the author of several books on complementary health care. She lives in Germany where she has a thriving complementary health practice.

CRYSTAL ENERGY

A
Practical
Guide to the Use
of Crystal Cards
for Rejuvenation
and Health
•

MONNICA HACKL

ELEMENT
Shaftesbury, Dorset ● Rockport, Massachusetts
Brisbane, Queensland

© 1993 F.A. Herbig Verlagbuchhandlung GmbH,
München

Published in Great Britain in 1994 by
Element Books Limited
Shaftesbury, Dorset

Published in the USA in 1994 by
Element, Inc.
42 Broadway, Rockport, MA 01966

Published in Australia in 1994 by
Element Books Limited for
Jacaranda Wiley Limited
33 Park Road, Milton, Brisbane 4064

Cover design by Peter Bridgewater Studios
Design by Roger Lightfoot
Typeset by Linda Reed and Joss Nizan
Printed and bound in Great Britain by
Redwood Books Ltd, Trowbridge, Wiltshire

British Library Cataloguing in Publication
data available

Library of Congress Cataloging in Publication
data available

ISBN 1–85230–590–8

CONTENTS

INTRODUCTION

ONE DAY a few years ago I was looking through the shelves in a small, dark, esoteric bookshop where the air smelled of aromatic herbs and incense. Suddenly, I became aware of a strong sensation to my left. I turned and saw a stand on which shiny cards of various colours were hanging. I reached out and touched a gold card, and instantly a wonderfully pleasant sensation ran up my arm.

This was the beginning of my relationship with crystal cards. I tried them out on myself and my family, and then eventually on my patients. The results they achieved convinced me that they are effective against a wide range of physical ailments, enhance the healing effects of other natural remedies and are a valuable tool for spiritual development.

Many people seem too busy to enjoy the simple pleasures of nature, or even food and drink, let alone take time to become healthy. Unfortunately, modern medical practice has led them to believe that the human body is just a machine. And when that machine does not seem to be functioning properly, orthodox medicine

1

relies on technical and mechanical means to mend it: doctors may prescribe aggressive chemicals, or remove and replace parts, just as if people were cars or computers. Chemical treatments quite often fail, a fast-acting drug might only suppress the symptoms temporarily, and the time required for a true recovery is often not taken into consideration. Even when modern medicines succeed initially, many patients have found that their effectiveness diminishes over time, so they must be taken in increasingly greater dosages.

It is, perhaps, not surprising that an ever-increasing number of people have begun to turn their attention back to remedies that come from nature and work with, not against, the natural rhythms of the human body. In the midst of our usually hectic existence, we need to pause; to put our life itself into perspective. Only when we commit ourselves to taking the time for both pleasure and health can we benefit from the natural healing powers of colours, crystals and flower essences.

These remedies might, at first, take longer to work than conventional medicines, but you do not need to worry about harmful side-effects. They work gently, surely and naturally. And although they may often work with amazing speed in cases of acute illness, they need time to be effective against more chronic ailments. The healthier you become, and the more sensitive you are to vibrations and the influences of a healthy lifestyle, the faster these gentle aids to health will work for you. Good health does not always mean having a constitution as strong as an ox; sometimes it means being sensitive and receptive to the often almost imperceptible influences that can affect the body's balance. This sensitivity helps us to recognize what disrupts our balanced functioning, and how to avoid it.

The book begins by discussing the effects of light and colour on the human body, and goes on to explain the healing powers of colour that can be absorbed through the body's energy centres. The introduction to the crystal cards includes the results of scientific studies and tests, and is followed by a chapter on some practical uses of the cards. There is also a chapter devoted to using the cards in conjunction with flower remedies. Then I share with you some of my experiences working with crystal cards, and invite you to enter the world of colour. The book concludes with an index of specific applications of the crystal cards.

1

COLOUR AND LIGHT

A S WE look around us, we notice that everything we can see has colour. Although we may be aware that we react to these colours in different ways, most of us probably do not realize that colours not only directly affect how we feel, physically and emotionally, but even how we behave. Thinking about it for a moment, you would probably agree that most people seem to feel better and are more cheerful on a bright, sunny day than on a gloomy, dull one. Similarly, you might have felt unhappy or depressed at some time, and then been cheered by the sight of a brightly coloured object. And perhaps you can remember standing in front of your wardrobe looking for just the right colour clothes for that day.

Light and colours, which are the different wavelengths of light, are perceived by the eyes and absorbed by the body through the skin and the optic nerves. They penetrate into the brain, where they are processed and utilized by the hypothalamus, the region of the brain that links the central nervous system to the hormonal system, and the light that penetrates to it at various wavelengths triggers a complex biochemical transfer within the body. When hormones and enzymes are exposed to coloured light, they themselves undergo changes in colour and begin to have different effects on the body. This is why people who are subjected to prolonged periods of darkness, during which their body cannot absorb any light, suffer from vitamin deficiencies, hormonal disorders, disturbances of the normal body cycles, particularly sleep and metabolic functions, and depression.

However, we are not totally dependent on our eyes to perceive light and colour. The ability to see without the use of one's eyes is known as eidetic ability. This means that 'looking' and 'seeing' take place exclusively in the brain, which creates strong mental images without the assistance of the optic nerves. Visions and the 'seeing' of the shamans are the result of this process. That colour and light can be 'seen' internally to a great extent without the aid of the retina is shown by the descriptions written by the Spanish saint Teresa of Avila in the sixteenth century, and by those of Eskimo shamans documented by the Danish explorer and ethnologist Knud Rasmussen in the early years of this century. The literature of mysticism, religion and anthropology contains many accounts of individuals' striking experiences of indescribable light, brilliant colours and the sense of multidimensional space, which remain invisible to onlookers. Such inner visions are often considered to be more impressive than mere optical sight, and seem to be experiences of such intensity that they remain vividly in the individual's mind for decades, and are rarely forgotten.

There is no dividing line between physical and emotional factors. Emotions are energies that can have direct effect on the body, its metabolism and its overall health.

Inner sight is not a sign of psychological abnormality, as was believed for a long time, but rather the sign of healthy stability and flexibility. The healthier an organism is, the more flexibly it responds to internal and external influences and stimuli. Experiments conducted in the former Soviet Union even investigated the possibility of perceiving colour solely with the sense of touch. What seemed impossible was actually achieved: several of the people tested were able to feel and 'see' – to correctly identify – colours through their fingertips.

That the human body is equipped with two 'safety systems' – eidetic sight and the sense of touch – to help it perceive light and colour without eyesight shows how important these elements are to our physical and emotional life.

Even if we should become blind, we retain the potential to avail ourselves, with some training, of the various qualities of light by these means.

THE AURA

Since ancient times there have been those who claim that we have, in addition to our physical body, other, etheric bodies, which they identify as vital, emotional, mental and causal bodies. Each of these etheric bodies has a counterpart in the physical body. If you find this concept difficult to accept, consider the phenomenon of so-called phantom pain, which is well known in orthodox medicine. This term refers to pain felt in a part of the body that has been amputated. Without the concept of etheric bodies there is no convincing explanation for phantom pain. However, if we accept the idea, we can assume that when we lose a physical limb, we retain its etheric equivalent. This is why Chinese medicine prescribes for such patients exercises that are to be performed as though the missing limb were present.

Modern biophysics has confirmed that human beings are composed not only of bone, muscle and tissue – mere physical matter – but also of a body of energy. Consisting of quanta of light, which are produced by every cell in the physical body, this body of energy thus corresponds to the etheric bodies identified by esoteric healers through the ages. One could say that every person is a rainbow, since everyone radiates his or her own colour vibrations, which form an aura, a sort of cocoon of etheric bodies enveloping the physical body. Located above the physical body's surface, this body of energy also ranks above it in terms of importance, since it directs and regulates everything that affects us.

All substances, environmental factors and living beings emit certain frequencies of energy. Those in our immediate environment are absorbed through our aura, the medium for the interaction of human and other energies, and directly affect us physically, emotionally and mentally. Sensitive individuals may even feel uncomfortable or unwell merely in the presence of people or other factors that emit a lower frequency: their own higher-frequency vibrations are drawn out and absorbed by the weaker source, leaving them drained and weak. It is also believed that all illness first appears in the etheric bodies and then slowly advances into the physical realm. For as long as an illness remains invisibly in the etheric bodies, it can be reached and removed only through vibrations. Therefore, whether or not we feel well, are healthy or ill, depends to a large extent on the health of our aura.

In order to become less susceptible to the ever-present external influences and to treat illnesses in the etheric bodies it is tremendously important to strengthen the aura. Combining colours with aluminium oxide crystals, whose structure enhances the effects of the colour, appears to be the ideal means by which to exert a stabilizing influence on our aura, and hence on our entire being.

2

CHAKRAS AND
COLOUR THERAPY

THE CHAKRAS are energy centres. Each of the seven chakras is associated with an area or organ of our physical body, and vibrates at a specific colour wavelength. This energy penetrates our physical form and emanates from there into infinity. Thus the chakras are the way in which spiritual information and life energy can reach the human body, and are the seat of our karma. By balancing and opening the chakras, we can moderate karmic patterns; with their help, we can grow beyond our basic instincts and attain higher planes of consciousness.

At one time the chakras were considered to be merely a theoretical aspect of Indian medicine. Today, however, it is possible to make the energy of the chakras, which radiates into the aura, visible by means of Kirlian photography. To trained therapists, pictures produced by this special high-voltage photographic technique clearly indicate any problems in our state of health.

THE SEVEN CHAKRAS

The first, and lowest, chakra, the base chakra, is located in the area of the perineum. Its colour is red. Red is a very hot colour, and in astrological terms corresponds to the signs of Scorpio and Aries. It is the colour of strength, sexuality and individuality.

The second chakra, the spleen or sacral chakra, is located in the sacral plexus. Its colour is orange, which is somewhat cooler than red, but still a hot colour. It is the colour of Leo, and stands for creative energy, intimacy and the release of fear.

The third chakra is that of the solar plexus. It is located about one inch above the navel and its colour is yellow. This colour corresponds to the sign of Libra and is associated with success, clear thinking, confidence and learning.

The fourth is the heart chakra, whose colour is green, the colour of the sign of Cancer, and of growth, harmony, love and balance.

The throat chakra is the fifth. Its colour is blue, which corresponds to the sign Capricorn and stands for communication, self-expression and peace.

The sixth chakra is the brow chakra, the so-called Third Eye, located between the eyebrows. Its colour, indigo, is that of Pisces, and represents wisdom, intuition and the release of habits.

The seventh, and highest, chakra is the crown chakra, located on top and a little towards the back of the head. Its colour is violet, the colour of Gemini, and of spirituality, love, healing, soul energy and calmness. (The colours of the sixth and seventh chakras vary depending on personality, ranging from violet to crimson, purple to indigo. It is therefore not possible to pinpoint a specific, consistent shade for either chakra.)

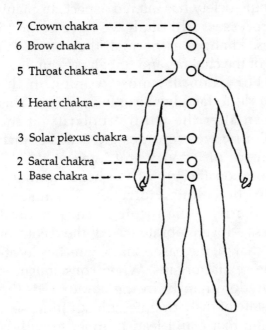

7 Crown chakra

6 Brow chakra

5 Throat chakra

4 Heart chakra

3 Solar plexus chakra

2 Sacral chakra

1 Base chakra

Fig.1 The location of the chakras in the human body

REVERSE POLARITY

The chakras must be kept in perfect balance in order for us to be totally healthy. Only then can we experience spiritual well-being and complete self-knowledge and self-understanding. However, the natural balance of the chakras can be disturbed when any of the wavelengths or vibrations is altered.

In its constant pursuit of technological progress, our society has altered aspects of many natural processes. Although we have come to accept these changes as normal, they affect the vibrations of the chakras and unbalance our energy field. For example, most women in the Western world today give birth lying down. This position can alter the natural polarity of the chakra colours; we were designed to be born with the force of gravity, not against it. The crown chakra on the top of the head normally vibrates in the colour violet, but because of reversed polarity – the result of an unnatural birth process – it can vibrate in red, the colour of the lowest chakra, the base chakra, which is located near the sexual organs. When consciousness vibrates predominantly in the colour red, the result is a state of disharmony with our inner self, and anything that could lead to inner growth is considered utterly irrelevant. Of course, not every horizontal birth results in this reversal of polarity, but it does happen all too often – we only need think of the sexual revolution of the 1960s.

COLOUR THERAPY

All of us have and need colour in our life. If you could see a person's aura with the naked eye, you would see how layer upon layer of energy envelops the body in the colours of the rainbow. There are an infinite number of colour vibrations in the world, but all of them are based on the seven main colours that vibrate in closest harmony with the body's organ centres, and so are associated with the chakras.

Since living things consist of colour, they can absorb colours purposefully and specifically. Just as the balance of the chakras can be disturbed by altering their natural vibrations, stimulating the chakras by means of corresponding colours markedly improves and balances their condition. By adjusting vibrations, colours can thus alleviate certain physical ailments and have a beneficial effect on our health.

Each chakra absorbs energy from the colour corresponding to it. When the colour is placed on the chakra, the wavelength of the colour harmonizes with it and causes it to expand. Chakras must be correctly stimulated and balanced: too much energy circulating through a chakra is just as undesirable as too little.

HARMONIZING THE CHAKRAS

The chakras are extremely powerful energy centres, and as such should be treated with the greatest respect. The correct stimulation of the base chakra increases the energy flow penetrating the body through the feet; this, in turn, activates smaller chakras in the feet. Opening the first chakra releases talents from previous lives, which can stabilize a person and enable him or her to develop character strength. The first chakra is associated with peace of mind, and is particularly closely tied to the etheric body; 'awakening' it promotes practical spiritual engagement. Red opens the base chakra; green closes it.

The second chakra is linked to the mental and emotional facilities. It is associated with creativity and initiative, as well as with the ability to deepen one's intimacy with others. Properly opened and balanced, the second chakra can reduce feelings of anger and make it easier for the individual to begin spiritual exercises. Orange opens it; blue closes it.

The mental sphere is linked to the third chakra, and the major symptom of imbalance here is depression. When balance is restored, so is one's emotional well-being, and feelings about one's mother, in particular, are resolved. Sensitivity and intuition may increase. Lemon yellow and gold open the third chakra; black closes it. People who have evolved spiritually use gold to open it.

The heart chakra acts as a great regularizer, and the astral, or emotional and spiritual bodies are connected to it. The attribute of divine love manifests itself in people whose fourth chakra has been awakened. Harmony and balance in all matters then have an opportunity to develop. A well-balanced fourth chakra helps all other chakras to link and unite. Emerald green and gold open it; orange closes it.

The throat chakra is closely linked to a well-integrated spiritual body. Stimulated, the fifth chakra promotes the development of self-expression. There is then a greater interest in spiritual matters, which arouses the same interest in others. People whose fifth chakra is closed tend to be introverted or morose, and are unable to express themselves emotionally. Blue and turquoise open this chakra; red, orange and yellow close it.

These five lower chakras influence us predominantly in terms of worldly matters. They have no influence on our free will with respect to our philosophy of life, personal vision or concept of God, or in relation to our personal choice of activities involving the higher powers.

17

The sixth chakra is related to the spiritual body and the soul. It stimulates the ability of creative visualization and the receptivity to visions. Insights deepen, as do inspiration and intuition. An unbalanced brow chakra results in withdrawal from reality. Indigo opens the chakra; red closes it.

The crown chakra stands in close relationship to the soul and is not associated with any negative emotions. A correctly stimulated seventh chakra results in a feeling of fulfilment or completeness, and a link to the higher powers. It renders intellect more spiritually oriented. Whereas the sixth chakra incorporates your ability to integrate God into your personal structure, the seventh relates to the eternal reality of God and shows you how you have integrated the higher powers. Violet, magenta and gold open it; black closes it.

In addition to the colours mentioned above, white opens all the chakras.

THE SEVEN RAYS

Meditating while the seven colours are applied to your chakras attunes your chakra energy to the seven rays. These are energies that work in and of themselves; they are powers of the soul. Every one of us relates most to one of these rays, which, in turn, reveals a great deal about our spiritual state, and about which mental and spiritual principles we have realized most thoroughly in our life.

- Red, the first ray, is creative and animating, and stands for spiritual power.
- Orange, the second ray, expresses and represents creative energy.
- The third ray is yellow. It completely transforms purely mental power, and it signifies understanding.
- Green, the colour of the fourth ray, brings the ability to transcend one's baser self, and represents harmony.
- The fifth ray is blue, and brings inner peace. It stands for peace.
- Indigo, the sixth ray, carries the ability to seek one's true self, and signifies wisdom.
- And, finally, violet, the seventh ray, creates a link between all of these abilities and the higher powers. It represents the perfect harmony of the entire spectrum of the six lower rays, and is marked by transcendental powers.

To enhance meditation, visualize each colour and dive into it. Start with the first ray, and continue to visualize the others in order. Practise this every morning for about three minutes before getting up.

PAINT A RAINBOW

Calmly painting a rainbow every day is another colour therapy that may have remarkable beneficial effects. Set aside ten minutes a day when you will not be disturbed by anyone or anything. Have a set of watercolours or felt-tip markers ready to use. Then start to paint a rainbow in the order of the chakra colours. You will notice that you practically thirst for some of the colours. If your mouth literally waters when you are using a particular colour, it is a clear sign that there is a deficiency of that colour vibration in your body at that time. Take your time in painting: sensitive people have found that even as they work with the seven colours of the rainbow the chakras in their etheric bodies begin to rebalance.

If you continue to paint daily, you will begin to feel emotionally stronger and calmer; later, you will experience additional inner harmony and clarity, and your physical energy will increase. This very simple method is well worth trying. Adults and children respond to it equally well, and children particularly derive immense pleasure from creating a rainbow every day.

3

CRYSTAL CARDS

CRYSTAL CARDS, which make use of the healing
power of colour with the special properties
of crystals, are a 'waste' by-product of American
space research. When exposed to mechanical
pressure, crystals emit electrons; they can store
information and their special structure makes
them well suited to programming. In space
research they were generally used to store
information.

American astronauts had noticed both physical
and psychological disorientation when leaving
the Earth's gravitational field. In an attempt to
take remedial action, the idea of using the properties of crystals was put forward. The astronauts
were given small containers with pyramid-
shaped crystals to take with them on their space
flights. The crystals were charged with the
Earth's mechanical vibration, which is 7.83 hertz.
The result was that the astronauts were able to
spend time outside the Earth's magnetic field
without suffering from their previous disorders.

Crystal cards are made of aluminium because it is a lightweight, soft metal that lends itself to the special, costly process of etching in the crystals. Thousands of microscopic, pyramid-shaped aluminium oxide crystals (corundum crystals) are etched into the cards by a complex electro-chemical process. By using naturally occurring minerals – tiny, live crystals – the cards become carriers of cosmic energy, which is enhanced by the pyramid shape. You can distinctly feel this energy through the skin and nervous system, through the chakras or other energy centres.

After being etched, the cards are coated with specific shades of non-toxic colours. The storage capabilities of the crystals are combined with the wavelengths of the colour vibrations, and the amplification of the effects of the colour through

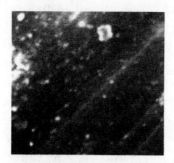

Fig. 2 A photograph of a crystal card taken with a scanning electron microscope before etching

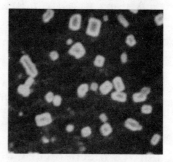

Fig. 3 A photograph of a crystal card taken with a scanning electron microscope after etching

the crystalline pyramids is what gives the cards their amazing power. The energy field of the cards also emits negative ions, which are vital for our well-being.

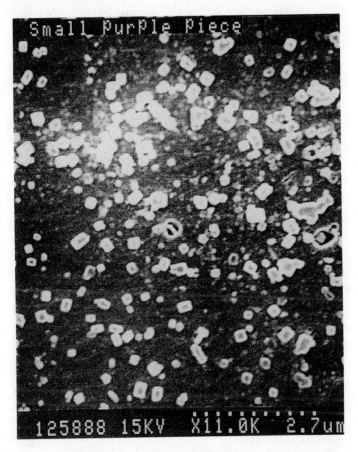

Fig. 4 A photograph of a violet card with crystals, greatly magnified

23

The cards are available in twenty colours, and are accompanied by information for their use in treating a range of physical and psychological ailments. Most crystal cards are the size and shape of a credit card, but some are equilateral triangles. Both types have the same effects on the body and are referred to as 'cards' in this book. They can be applied to specific parts of the body, carried in a wallet or pocket, or used to energize food or drink.

THE PENDULUM TEST

Each card has a positive and a negative side. To identify the sides you will need a simple pendulum, such as a needle suspended on a cotton thread. Place the card on a table in front of you and suspend the pendulum over the centre of it. Rest your elbows on the tabletop to be sure that the pendulum is not influenced by your own movements. If the pendulum circles clockwise above the card, the side facing up is positive; if it circles anticlockwise, the side facing up is negative. Positive and negative are not associated with good and bad in this context, but describe a physical process or property: the vibrations of the positive side create input, while the negative side extracts vibrations.

If you continue to hold the pendulum above

the card, you will notice that after a while it will stop circling in the initial direction and begin moving the other way. The process reverses again after another few minutes. This proves that there really are pyramid-shaped crystals etched into the card, as radiesthetic tests have detected alternating reversing circular vibrations above pyramids in general. Use only the direction of the first swing to mark the crystal card. It is a good idea to mark the negative side, which should face towards the body in most cases and for most purposes.

SCIENTIFIC TESTS

A physicist at 21st Century Technologies, a research and development institute in Waterford, Connecticut, has examined the crystal cards with the requisite scientific scepticism. To his surprise, he found that the cards act as molecular negative-ion generators, and are able to generate a magnetic field equivalent to 9000 gauss. His report explains:

> A basic idea in neurometrics and radionics is that each organism or material radiates and absorbs energy through a unique wave field, which exhibits certain geometrical, frequency and radiation-type characteristics. This is an extended force field that exists around all forms of matter, whether animate

25

*Fig. 5 A Kirlian photograph
of a finger before a crystal card
was held*

or inanimate. The more complex the material, the more complex the wave-form.

I believe the fundamental carrier wave [of the cards] is polarized with a rotating polarization vector. The information concerning the glands and body systems ripples the carrier wave and seems to be associated with a specific phase modulation of the wave for a specific gland. Regions of space associated with a given phase angle of the wave constitute a three-dimensional network of points extending through space. To be in resonance with any one of these points is to be in resonance with the particular gland of the entity.

It is possible to scan the wave-form of the gland to detect any abnormalities (neurometrics). If energy having the normal or healthy wave-form of the gland is pumped into any of the specific network points, the gland will be driven in the normal or healthy mode. This produces a tendency for its structure to reorganize itself in close alignment with the normal pattern, i.e., healing of the gland

26

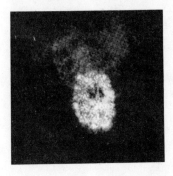

Fig. 6 A Kirlian photograph of the same finger after a violet crystal card was held for one minute; the energy field surrounding the finger is noticeably larger.

occurs. Cells born in this polarizing field tend to grow in a healthier configuration, which weakens the diseased or abnormal structure and strengthens the healthy or normal one. It is my opinion that continued exposure to these cards could promote normal, healthy development in the human body.

Radiation intensity and frequency

The capabilities of the crystal cards were also tested in a Swiss research institute. The colours tested were gold, black, violet, turquoise and silver. Each card was measured eight times, once for each alignment with the eight points of the compass: north, north-east, north-west, south, south-east, south-west, east and west.

Table 1 shows that the radiation, or emission, intensity (R) and the emission frequency (F) vary with the alignment of the card. The variations in

Card	Horizontal emissions		Horizontal, energy drawn in by lateral sides				Vertical positions Radiation, by active lateral side 'A'*							
	R	F	a	b	c	d	S	SW	W	NW	N	NE	E	SE
Gold	15	9	-7	-8	-6	-8	21, 8.9	21, 9.1	21, 9.2	22, 9.0	24, 8.8	21, 9.2	21, 9.0	22, 9.0
Black	23	9.5	-12	-8	-12	-9	25, 9.6	24, 9.5	26, 9.3	23, 9.1	22, 9.0	21, 9.4	22, 9.5	24, 9.6
Violet	33	8.5	-15	-18	-15	-14	26, 8.1	28, 7.9	30, 7.7	33, 7.5	34, 4.6	31, 8.4	34, 9.0	32, 9.4
Turquoise	26	10.2	-8	-9-	-8	-9	23, 10.3	26, 10.3	27, 10.2	27, 10.1	26, 10.0	27, 9.9	28, 9.8	24, 9.8
Silver	28	10.4	-7	-6	-9	-6	30, 10.2	31, 10.3	27, 10.2	24, 10.1	23, 10.3	22, 10.5	21, 10.5	22, 10.3

R: radiation (emission) intensity
F: radiation frequency or quality
*The first number in each pair is radiation intensity, the second number is radiation frequency

Table 1 Energy emission levels of five important crystal cards

intensity are minor; alignment has an influence of only 1 or 2 per cent. Emission frequency represents the quality of radiation. It is surprising that gold, which represents total protection, corresponds to the frequency of human life energy, which is 9.1 ± 2 per cent. Black facing north-east corresponds to the frequency of the heart chakra at 9.4; and turquoise and silver facing in several directions correspond to the frequency of the brow chakra of 10.3. In this experiment violet exhibited the greatest emission intensity, coupled with a relatively low frequency. Violet grows out of, and surpasses, the vibration of life energy.

The engineer responsible, who is also a naturopath, confirmed that the colours gold and black in particular protect against technologically produced radiation, such as that which builds up during work at a computer or photocopier, or during long journeys in trains and cars. His studies also found the silver, gold and black cards to be helpful in protecting people who administer health care to others. Of course, people who are not well should – indeed, must – rid themselves of negative vibrations in the course of treatment; after all, that is the point of therapy. Sensitive care-givers, however, can absorb these discarded low-frequency vibrations, which may be exhausting, illness-producing energies. Silver, gold and black prevent the absorption of these negative energies, and help the body gradually to attain a stable resonance, which, in time, will make it less susceptible to this kind of external vibration.

Further tests on the crystal cards were made in Austria, where Werner H. Duschnig performed a radiesthetic test. He, too, found that the edges of the cards, which are only one millimetre thick, draw in energy from their surroundings, and that this energy is then released through the active (positive) flat side, or face, of the cards. If you were to be too close to the edge of a card, or the side of a stack of cards, for too long, it could reduce your own energy levels. However, you could use the energy that is released again through the active card face to help build up the body's energy fields and structures.

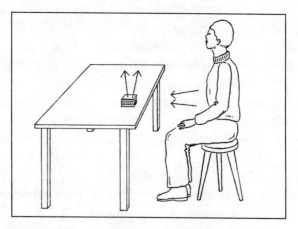

Fig. 7 Energy is drawn in by the narrow edges of the cards. When carrying a crystal card, always make sure that one flat side is in contact with the body.

Test report

Test object
Crystal cards, chakra set

Test conditions
The tests were conducted at a location approximating neutral geopathic conditions. Any potentially disruptive fields generated by electrical cables and instruments or appliances were eliminated as far as possible.

Each test object was measured in two positions:
1 horizontally, lying flat on the table, and
2 vertically, fitted into a holding device that permits the object to be aligned with the various points of the compass. In particular, the stability of emission frequency relative to compass alignment was measured in this position.

Radiation intensity (R) and the corresponding frequency (F) were measured in both positions.

Definitions
The concept of radiation (emission) is borrowed from physics, as this phenomenon has similar properties.
    Frequency is another familiar concept, which is used to describe the second aspect of the energetic phenomenon being measured.
    The terms 'life energy' and 'human energy' are to be found in the subject literature. Every living thing – plants, animals and humans – has its species-specific 'radiation', which falls within a characteristic range of

31

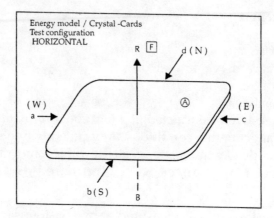

Fig. 8 Horizontal test configuration; the crystal card draws in energy through its edges (a, b, c, d), and through its negative side, B. It radiates energy (R) from the positive, or active, side, A. The card is aligned precisely along the north-south axis.

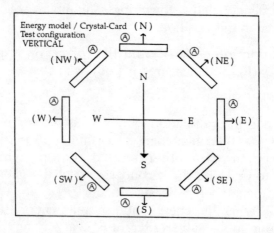

Fig. 9 Vertical test configuration for all eight major points of the compass

frequencies. In this report the range of frequencies, or frequency band, is termed the range of life energy, and extends from 7.25 to 11.47 units. The emissions of the individual chakras and their specific frequencies fall within this band.

At 9.15, the radiation of the human body falls in about the middle of the frequency band of life energy, and in this report is called 'human energy'.

The units of radiation (R) and frequency (F) used in the report represent individual, non-standardized quantities.

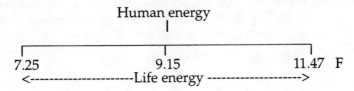

Human energy

7.25	9.15	11.47 F

<------------------------Life energy --------------------->

Fig. 10 The life energy range

General comments
All test objects exhibit the typical characteristics of one neutral side and two active areas:
1 Energy is drawn into the object laterally (negative emissions a–d); this factor is irrelevant to the purpose and use of crystals cards.
2 The energy drawn in laterally is emitted in intensified form by the active axial side, 'A', opposite the neutral side.

The frequencies of the individual chakras are matched with astonishing precision, especially in the horizontal position. The corresponding radiation emission seems to be strong enough so that when the products (the crystal cards) are applied directly to the body they can achieve a harmonizing effect on the various chakras. However, it seems that this influence becomes possible only when the active side is facing the chakras.

Therefore, for effective use of this product, it is absolutely necessary that the cards be appropriately marked or labelled, and that detailed instructions accompany them. Determining the active side by means of pendulum dowsing by the user, as suggested in the instructions, is absolutely not recommended.

In the set of test objects provided for this examination the colours of the heart chakra and the brow chakra were clearly mixed up.

Product description
- Red: horizontally, red radiates in the frequency of the base chakra; vertically, this frequency is attained when the active side faces north-west.
- Orange: horizontally, orange radiates in the frequency of the sacral chakra; vertically, this frequency is attained when the active side faces north.
- Yellow: horizontally, yellow radiates in the frequency of the solar plexus chakra; vertically, this frequency is attained when the active side faces south-west or south-east.
- Green: horizontally, green radiates in the frequency of the brow chakra; vertically, this frequency is attained when the active side faces west or south-west.
- Blue: horizontally, blue radiates in the frequency of

Card	Horizontal		F, vertical								R, vertical
	R	F	S	SW	W	NW	N	NE	E	SE	—
Red	14	7.65	8.20	—	8.70	7.65	7.20	—	7.00	—	27
Orange	21	8.45	8.20	—	7.60	—	8.45	—	8.70	—	33
Yellow	33	8.73	9.00	8.73	8.6	—	8.20	—	8.00	8.73	37
Green	29	10.23	10.00	—	10.23	—	11.00	—	10.40	10.23	33
Blue	29	9.70	9.80	9.70	9.40	—	9.70	—	10.00	—	35
Indigo	32	9.40	9.60	—	9.40	—	9.20	—	9.40	—	40
Violet	26	10.80	11.20	10.80	10.20	—	10.40	—	10.60	—	44

Table 2 Test results for the seven chakra colours of crystal cards

the throat chakra; vertically, this frequency is attained when the active side faces south-west or north.

- Indigo: horizontally, indigo radiates in the frequency of the heart chakra; vertically, this frequency is attained when the active side faces west or east.
- Violet: horizontally, violet radiates in the frequency of the crown chakra; vertically, this frequency is attained when the active side faces south-west.

Conclusions

As already mentioned, the accuracy of frequency matching is especially remarkable when the test objects are horizontal. Labelling the active side of each card, and the provision of detailed instructions for use are desirable. The switch in the colours for the heart and brow chakras, possibly an error that occurred during manufacturing, must be corrected.

Werner H. Duschnig
Vienna, 29 August 1992

Duschnig, who performed these tests with great precision, did not have an opportunity to reproduce his findings. Nevertheless, it seems justified to include them here, since they show impressively just how accurately the crystal cards correspond to the vibrations of the individual human chakras.

It is important to clarify the discrepancies that Duschnig appeared to find. The green card, which bears the colour of the heart chakra, was measured as radiating at the same frequency as the brow chakra, whose colour is indigo. Similarly, the indigo card exhibited the frequency of the heart chakra. Duschnig assumed that a mistake had been made in the manufacture of the cards he tested. I believe that there may be another explanation. Our feelings are often superseded and stifled by our thoughts – our heart and common sense often tell us very different things, and many of us have suffered from being torn between, for example, our heart saying yes and our mind saying no. So it might be that the frequencies of the heart and brow are responsible for balancing and aligning these two conflicting centres in order to decrease the gap between emotion and intellect.

And although Duschnig rejects the idea that the positive and negative sides of the cards may be determined by dowsing with a pendulum, experience shows that even people doing this for the first time are successful. I have asked a considerable number of people to try the pendulum test, and, to the great surprise of every one of them, the pendulum moved in more or less well-defined circles. The size of the circles is unimportant, and reflects only the person's dowsing ability. You too can use this easy test to identify the active side of crystal cards and triangles.

4

SOME PRACTICAL APPLICATIONS OF CRYSTAL CARDS

CRYSTAL CARDS work with the natural energies of your body. They do not heal you by themselves, but they activate the body's natural energies, and assist and support them with their own energy. The colour of the card guides both organs and emotions back to their correct vibrations. The crystalline structure stimulates the energy centres far more effectively than the colour alone could, not only by rendering the colour denser, but also by activating the chakra's etheric and astral tones. In this way the body's own energy is channelled into the ailing part.

Carrying natural quartz, or rock, crystals has become very popular. When you carry crystal cards together with quartz crystals, the energy of the quartz crystals is amplified. For the best results with this combination, it is recommended that you wear polished rock crystal spheres and carry the crystal card in a pocket.

Because crystal cards produce an energy vortex. it does not matter whether the positive or negative side faces up when energizing food and drinks. However, it is important to carry the card with the negative side facing your body when you want to draw out something negative, and to carry it with the positive side towards you when you want to channel in positive energy.

It is essential that you use the correct colour – it must correspond to the organ to be influenced – in order for the healing process to succeed. Whatever colour is used, you must apply the card consistently to the area that it is to affect in order to change the vibrations there. If you use the card only occasionally, there will not be a great deal of progress. You need to give your body time to recharge its energies. However, it is not necessary to carry a card with you for months on end. After a period of time, the ailment will have diminished to a point where you can put away the card. You can use it again if a new need arises.

CARD CARE

After every use, and certainly before you lend your crystal card to another person, be sure to rinse it thoroughly with cold, running water, and then expose it to light and fresh air. This ensures that the next user will not pick up any foreign vibrations that might be stored in the crystals from the last time the card was used.

TESTING

There are two simple ways to determine which card or cards you need to use. The first is the muscle test, commonly used in kinesiology. Stand holding the crystal card to be tested in your hand, with your arm stretched out at shoulder level. Have a partner press down gently on your arm. If you can resist the pressure, the colour is right for you. If your arm becomes weak and is pushed down, you and the card are incompatible.

The second way is to use a pendulum. Hold the card a little distance in front of you at chest level. Ask your test partner to suspend the pendulum between you and the card. If the pendulum begins to swing back and forth in a connecting direction between you and the card, you need the energy emitted by that card. If the pendulum swings in a dividing direction – that is, parallel to you and the card – you do not need the card.

BALANCING POLARITY

Before vibrations can be changed by using crystal cards, you must balance your polarity. Place the violet card on top of your head, and the red card on your sexual organs daily for ten to fifteen minutes. After only one week you will notice a difference. Your overall sense of life will be clearer, and the purpose and direction of your own life will become distinct, and your concentration span and ability will increase.

THE COLOUR KIT

The Colour Kit consists of seven small triangles, of the same material as the crystal cards, in the colours of the seven major chakras. Each triangle is small enough to be worn like a piece of jewellery, suspended from a chain threaded through the small hole pierced in one point. This way it can be worn over whichever part of the body is to be treated. Used together with the techniques of meditation, the Colour Kit opens and balances the seven major chakras and tunes in to their colour vibrations. The Colour Kit also enhances the natural process by which the chakras balance themselves while you sleep.

You can also use the Colour Kit to 'brush' your aura to remove energy blockages. For the best results brush the aura with the red, green, blue and violet triangles separately. Hold the triangle in your left hand and brush it systematically across your entire body area, up and down, left and right, at a distance of two to four inches from the body surface; in this way you remain within the energy field of your aura.

Before using the Colour Kit, identify each colour triangle with the chakra to which it corresponds. Cleanse the triangles frequently by rinsing them under cold, running water for about thirty seconds.

THE CHAKRA CRYSTAL CARDS

Red

The red crystal card is particularly good for people who are subjected to intense stress. Managers, entrepreneurs and other people who take an active part in stressful business life all day long, day in and day out, have reported good results with red. After carrying this card with them for a few days, they felt strengthened and considerably calmer. So red is for active people, who are not stimulated by it – as more sensitive people are – but instead are calmed down.

If you have low blood pressure, reach for the red card only if you are, on the whole, an active and dynamic person. Delicate and sensitive people with low blood pressure are better off carrying the green crystal card. If you are not sure which of these crystal colours is appropriate for you, put the red card against the palm of your hand and hold it to your chest, flat against your skin. Walk around like this for about five minutes. If you notice any inner disquiet, heart palpitations or shortness of breath while doing this, then red is not right for you. (The crystal card does not even have to be removed from its plastic packaging for this test to work.) However, even if you can tolerate the red crystal card very well, do not carry it too high on your body. It is much better to carry it in your belt or in a skirt or trouser pocket than in a shirt pocket.

Many people benefit from red when they suffer from coughing, lack of energy, and bladder problems. Carry red with you too if you suffer from arthritis; it helps to channel energy into the joints, which seem to regenerate themselves.

Do not use red during puberty. This colour relates to sexual energy and during puberty – a period of excess sexual energy – this factor should not be enhanced.

Orange

Orange has a stimulating effect, and promotes the expression of creative energy. It helps you to become more energetic, to develop intimacy and to release fear. It is also helpful in cases of alcohol or drug addiction. When you carry orange with you, you feel as safe and secure as in a warm bath.

Orange is a colour for the physical body too. It is used to combat sore throat, muscle weakness and stomach pain. Placing an orange card into your shoes can help in cases of athlete's foot.

Yellow

This card, which is the colour of the sun and has effects similar to sunlight, helps moody people to concentrate and balance their energies. If there are disturbances of the brain tissues, the yellow card helps the dysfunctional part of the brain, and directs connective impulses to the healthier parts. To help reduce fever, place yellow cards against the nape of the neck and on the forehead, with the positive side touching the skin.

Yellow is very important for children in particular: energize their drinking water with it for twelve to fourteen minutes. Placing the card on your desk after using it to energize drinking water is very beneficial too: the stimulating, concentration-enhancing effect of the card is noticeable even at a little distance.

The effects of the yellow card are so strong that some people can tolerate it near their body for only short periods of time. If the card is carried in a shirt or trouser pocket for more than twenty to thirty minutes, sensitive individuals begin to experience heart palpitations and restlessness. It is advisable, therefore, not to carry yellow in direct contact with the body for more than twenty minutes, and never to carry it anywhere on the chest at heart level. The area of the solar plexus, between the lower end of the sternum (breastbone) and the navel, is the highest point for the yellow card. The lower belly, between the navel and the pubic bone, is also a good place to apply this card.

Green

Green initiates the healing process. Many people use this card to treat bruises, kidney trouble and kidney stones, and even for the elimination of toxicity in the body.

Urban drinking water is full of chemicals. Place a glass of water on the green card for fifteen minutes and drink some of it three times a day, three days a week. You can help make acne disappear by drinking water energized with green and by washing the problem areas with it, and by placing the card on the affected skin area. Water energized with green can also be used for washing hands or feet affected by fungal infections, such as athlete's foot.

Blue

Blue channels positive energy, and relaxes. It is useful against bleeding, burns and underweight. It brings inner peace and is helpful for people who are tired at the end of a long day at work. Its energy is cool and refreshing, and at the same time balancing; it is a wonderful gift to a young mother and her newborn child.

Indigo

Indigo is the vibration of the masters. It promotes wisdom and intuition, and makes it easier for people to break old behavioural patterns or bad habits. It channels energy directly into the body, and, used in conjunction with other cards, it helps to regenerate worn-out joints.

Violet

Violet is the colour of higher consciousness, and gradually builds up inner peace. It links the chakras to each other and, along with indigo, is the card for the 'Third Eye'. Violet and the lighter shade of lavender help to bring the various etheric bodies into accord with each other and to balance shifts in alignment within them. Often, the correction of misalignments in the etheric realm is the prerequisite for permanent relief of ailments.

Placing the violet card on your head reduces mental fears; when positioned behind the ear, it effects mental and spiritual balance. Use violet to help alleviate toothache, combat allergies and to help generally after an operation. If your feet hurt when you get up in the morning, stand on two violet cards for a few minutes to stimulate your circulation.

Many people report that violet helps against ageing skin, back pain, and stress, and that it produces good results in helping treat nappy rash, insomnia, water retention and varicose veins. Carry the violet card with you if you are easily irritated by smoke. Some therapists recommend using violet to reduce the tension that can lead to alcohol and drug abuse, and astrologists use it to counteract the effects of retrograde planets.

SOME OTHER COLOURS

Black

Use black to protect yourself against radiation from computers, microwave ovens, electrical outlets and all the negative or electrical energies in your home. Computers and many other kinds of electrical equipment drain the energy field and produce positive ions. You may have experienced the uncomfortable atmosphere in a large office where a great deal of electrical equipment – computers, photocopiers, fax machines – was operating at the same time, or in an electronics shop where fifty or more televisions were on simultaneously. Because of an excess of positively charged ions in such places, a condition known as electrosmog, the air is very dry and electrically charged, and it is possible to get minor electric shocks when touching objects.

People who have been exposed to electrosmog frequently or for long periods of time report that they suffer increasingly from irritability and nervousness, depression and fatigue. Their skin becomes dry, their eyes sore, and they get headaches and allergic reactions.

Now recall a day you spent in the open country, in a forest, in the mountains, along a river or on a lake. Remember how well you felt there? Negatively charged ions predominate in natural surroundings. They are the reason why we feel – and are – healthier, refreshed and balanced there. These negative ions are at their most intense near waterfalls or ocean surf. The countless fog-like water droplets disperse them through the air, which is why so many people find it calming and regenerating to be on the beach.

Black rids people of negative energy, which can manifest itself as tension or depression, and allows positive thinking patterns to develop. The black card absorbs negative energy, disperses subconscious 'blocks' and reduces stress. It removes harmful rays and absorbs radiation. In the future it will be used to cleanse foods of radiation residue. This colour also closes the seventh chakra.

Gold

Gold stands for prosperity, power and total protection. It brings out the positive in you, and prevents negative energy from entering the body. This card should be carried as close to the body as possible.

Whatever life has intended for you, gold makes it manifest and draws it towards you. Set a clear quartz crystal (rock crystal) on the gold card and watch what happens. A whole host of circumstances and events you have always wished for will come into your life, whether they be promising business opportunities or satisfying interpersonal experiences.

I have noticed that this combination, which is best set up on a windowsill so that plenty of light can reach it, works so clearly and powerfully that it makes some people uneasy. The effects of this seemingly magical spell can be so pronounced that they are, in fact, tempted to dismantle the arrangement. This is because, for these individuals, it is stressful to be faced with positive events and the fulfilment of their wishes. They can no longer complain that life has denied them their chance, and they are challenged to make use of their potential.

Pink

Pink enhances self-confidence and helps us to be forgiving and loving. It is the colour that helps to externalize problems, and is especially useful to those people who need to learn that one must first love oneself before being able to love others. It is also a colour to use to support the healing process in cases of cancer; simply place the card on the skin.

Sky blue

Sky blue works gently on releasing you from habits buried deep in your past or in your karma. A process such as this has its price, and headaches are a common side-effect. I suggest you carry this card for only one or two hours initially, gradually extending the time. Always remove the card at the first sign of a headache. Some people report that sky blue works particularly well when gently placed beneath one's pillow overnight.

The blue gemstone sodalite has a similar effect, erasing old and karmic patterns, and some people have noticed that they develop a headache when they wear a sodalite necklace, just as they do when they carry the sky blue crystal card.

COMBINATIONS OF COLOURS

- Red and blue are helpful for sinus trouble. Put one card on each sinus, with the negative side of each card touching the skin. Switch the cards after ten minutes
- Use the yellow and orange cards to stimulate your pancreas. Place the cards, with the positive sides towards your skin, about four fingers' breadth above and a little to the left of the navel. Place the orange card diagonally on the skin, and the yellow card crossways on top of it. Do this for three days to allow the colours to penetrate into the body, then stop.
- Yellow and indigo are the colours to use in all cases of infection, particularly fungal infections. Place both cards in hot water, and use the water to wash your feet.
- Yellow and violet are helpful against toothache.
- For various types of congestion, place green on the nape of the neck to initiate the healing process. Place orange on the left shoulder blade and violet on the right shoulder blade. The negative side of all the cards should face the body. After ten minutes, switch the orange and violet cards.

- Use blue and yellow to combat colds, and blue and green to help treat sprains.
- For pulled muscles, apply violet first to soothe the pain, then bandage up with green on one side and blue on the other. Switch the blue and green after twenty minutes.
- People with high blood pressure should place blue and green cards on either side of the chest, with the positive sides facing away from the body. Switch after ten minutes.
- To make the stress of puberty easier carry blue, indigo and violet cards, and do *not* use red.
- Indigo and gold can help to break destructive eating habits, and thus can be used to help you lose weight or stop smoking. The same combination is helpful in asthma cases.
- To heighten your learning abilities, carry violet and yellow: the violet soothes restlessness and disquiet, which can interfere with concentration and learning, and yellow boosts alertness and concentration.
- Use violet and silver to help combat pain. Place the negative side of the violet card against your skin, and then put the silver card, positive side down, crossways on top of the violet.
- Carry violet and black cards together in the same pocket to combat depression. This combination particularly helps people who tend to place the blame for circumstances on themselves or others.

- If you want to remember your dreams, place violet and gold cards under your pillow.
- It is recommended that people who suffer from severe stress but cannot tolerate red should carry violet and blue cards. The same combination may also help ease labour pains.
- If you feel negative, you might find it beneficial to use gold and black together; they balance the energies. Carry the two cards with you in your pockets – it does not matter whether the positive or negative sides face your body.

ENERGIZING FOOD AND DRINK

- A rough or sore throat indicates a disturbance, a sort of congestion, in the area of the throat chakra. Drinking water energized with the blue card will help to alleviate the organic symptoms.
- Before mealtimes place children's food on the indigo card, and their drinks on the violet.To energize their drinking water, place it on the yellow card for twelve to fourteen minutes. Drinks energized with the extremely stimulating yellow card can be drunk without worry, but not more than about one glass a day
- To eliminate harmful substances, set a glass of drinking water on the violet card. Place the violet card underneath all alcoholic beverages to greatly reduce the effects of the alcohol.

- When you want to feel refreshed, put your drinks on the orange card for ten minutes.
- Never use black for energizing water.

TREATMENT FOR BACK PAIN

If you suffer from back pain due to spinal misalignment, lie face down with your head pointing north and your feet south. Place the orange card on the lower end of the spine, the green card somewhat higher up, indigo on the nape of the neck and violet on the back of the neck, all with the negative sides facing the body. Leave the cards in place for ten minutes.

A second combination you can try is black at the base of the spine, and orange, green and red in the other positions, again with the negative side of the cards facing the body, so that the pain is drawn out and returned to the universe.

PLANTS AND ANIMALS

Everything on Earth vibrates in colour wavelengths, just like the human body. If you use medicinal herbs, you will notice even better effects if you combine them with the colours matching their vibrations, because this helps the body to assimilate them more quickly. For example, use green with alfalfa and dandelion, blue with aloe, turquoise with eyebright, yellow with catmint, and yellow or violet with chamomile.

Place a clear glass bottle of water on the green card and give this water to plants, especially weak or sickly ones – you will be surprised at how quickly they recover. If you want to go one step further, you can bury one or two aventurine crystals in the soil (more for trees). Like green, these stones also represent growth and healing, and people in need of a healing influence should wear a necklace of slightly transparent aventurine stones for several months.

Animals vibrate in three major chakras: the base chakra, which is red; the heart chakra, green; and the crown chakra, indigo. Because we are constantly subjected to a great deal of stress against which we often have no defences, we transfer this tension to the animals around us. Whether they are agricultural livestock or pets, colours can help them to cope with their environment.

When using crystal cards to benefit animals, always use silver as the main colour, as it represents Mother Earth herself. Only then can other colours and combinations be used, such as red or blue for arthritis, black and violet for despondency, or violet for overly aggressive or restless behaviour. Remember that, as for humans, the cards must be applied consistently to the area they are to affect in order to change the vibrations there.

5

FLOWER REMEDIES AND CRYSTAL CARDS

FLOWER REMEDIES were developed by Dr Edward Bach, an English physician, in the early part of this century. After practising as a consultant for a number of years, Dr Bach became a research bacteriologist, and earned an impressive reputation for his work. However, as his work progressed, he became more and more disenchanted with the care he could give his patients by exclusively orthodox medical means, and so he turned to homoeopathy.

Working at the Royal London Homoeopathic Hospital, Dr Bach developed seven nosodes (a kind of homoeopathic vaccine) for chronic diseases, which bear his name and are still in use today. But even this did not satisfy him, so he gave up his busy clinic and moved out to the country. There, in the course of years of research, he discovered the so-called flower essences, which are now used by therapists in many countries throughout the world.

Dr Bach classified thirty-eight flowers to be used to treat the negative states of mind from which people can suffer. He realized that the defining symptom of an illness is not the name or description of the disease itself, such as scarlet fever or influenza, but its unique manifestation in each patient. He found that patients with the same psychological symptoms responded to the same treatment regardless of their physical ailments, and that patients suffering from the same physical illness were cured by treatment with different flower remedies. Thus three children suffering from the same illness – say, whooping cough – may be given three completely different flower essences to achieve a cure. Prescription is guided by the psychological characteristics each child displays. Young Jack, for example, exhibits a marked fear during his coughing attacks, so he is given the essence of mimulus. His sister Anne, however, complains of a dull, stuffy feeling in her head, and so hornbeam is the flower prescribed for her. And Michael, a friend of Jack and Anne who also has the illness, acts in an unusually bossy manner, and is given vine.

ADDING COLOUR

As I sit here looking out the window at the marvellous spring flowers and the delicate pink-and-white blossoms on the apple trees, it is, first and foremost, the colours that delight me. One of Dr Bach's practices was to transfer the essence of such colourful blooms into pure spring water through the power of sunlight. The relationship between flower remedies and colour therapy is as plain and simple as nature itself: there is no blossom without colour, and colours, as we have seen, can affect our moods and state of mind as well as our physical health. Therefore, it would seem clear that combining the flower essences with colours could enhance both these methods of natural healing.

Table 3 shows the seven categories into which Dr Bach divided his remedies, and the colours associated with them by other practitioners. I have tested the links between the flower essences and the colours, and found that an exceptional proportion of my patients chose the colours that corresponded to the flower essences they needed for their treatment.

Before using the flower remedies it is essential to have your symptoms assessed by a qualified practitioner. Then you can augment your treatment with red, orange, yellow, green, turquoise, blue and violet, which correspond almost exactly

Characteristic	Flower remedy	Colour
Fear	Aspen Cherry plum Mimulus Red chestnut Rock rose	Yellow
Insecurity	Cerato Gentian Gorse Hornbeam Scleranthus Wild oat	Red
Lack of interest in present circumstances	Clematis Honeysuckle Wild rose Chestnut bud Mustard Olive White chestnut	Yellow Turquoise
Loneliness	Heather Impatiens Water violet	Green
Hypersensitivity	Agrimony Centaury Holly Walnut	Blue
Despondency or despair	Crab apple Elm Larch Oak Pine Star of Bethlehem Sweet Chestnut Willow	Violet Orange
Excessive worrying about the welfare of others	Beech Chicory Rock water Vervain Vine	Green

Table 3 Flower remedies and corresponding colours
(Based on I.S.Kraaze and W.von Ruhr, Die richtige Schwingung heilt)

to the colours of the rainbow, the seven major chakras and the basic healing colours.

USING THE CRYSTAL CARDS

Each flower essence and each crystal card work on specific vibrational levels. By using them together, the levels combine to form new energy fields that support the healing process. For example, let's say that you are suffering from exhaustion and need the essence of olive. This is normally not a fast-acting cure, but if you add a few drops to a glass of water and place the glass on the crystal card of the corresponding colour – turquoise – for about twenty minutes, you will feel the strengthening effect of the mixture after only a few drinks. In these circumstances it usually is not necessary to take the drops for more than one day unless the problem is very deep-seated.

Another way of combining the two therapies is to carry the appropriate colour crystal card or apply it directly to the affected part of your body at the same time as using the flower remedy. You can carry all the cards except the yellow in a shirt, skirt or trouser pocket all day long. However, do not allow any of them to be in contact with your skin for more than thirty minutes. It is also important to remember that the red and yellow cards should never be applied to, or carried at, heart or upper chest level.

Yellow

Yellow corresponds to the flower remedies for fear and a lack of interest in the present. People suffering from these conditions need a 'spark' to jolt them out of their mental tension or lethargy. Combined with crystal energy, the powerful colour yellow can provide the necessary impetus. It is so very stimulating, however, that even if it is not in direct contact with the body, it should not be carried for more than twenty minutes at the most; longer than this and sensitive people, in particular, may begin to experience heart palpitations and nervousness.

Violet

The flower essence of crab apple is the only remedy corresponding to the colour violet. Crab apple is known as the cleansing flower; according to Dr Bach it is capable of gradually removing toxins, germs, deposits and metabolic waste products from the body. Violet is said to have similar effects in the etheric bodies.

As we have seen through the example of phantom pain, the etheric bodies appear to have a counterpart to every part of the physical body.

Injury to an etheric component results in physical pain, and physical or emotional trauma can cause the etheric counterparts to shift. Blockages or congestion in the etheric bodies can hinder or prevent a return to perfect health.

Imagine for a moment that you can see all the etheric bodies with your naked eye. At first glance, you see a person in the usual way, but when you look more closely, you see the first layer of the aura as a shining light enveloping the body about an inch above its surface. This is the layer that can be seen and recorded by Kirlian photography; it is the only layer of the aura to be scientifically verified.

Although there is no scientific proof for the existence of the other layers of the aura that have been described by esoteric therapists, they say the second layer, which is some eight inches deep, is the emotional body. Emotional experiences become encoded here, and often create blockages. Next comes the mental body, which reacts to thoughts received or generated by the person, and beyond that is the causal body, which holds the individual's potential for future development.

It is easy to see that healing will be quickest and most complete if all the parts of the physical body are represented in the same location in all four layers of the aura. However, physical ailments, accidents, emotional and mental problems and other traumas cause the representations of the physical body to shift, to misalign in respect to each other, in the etheric bodies. Let us imagine, for example, that an acupuncturist inserts a needle to detoxify the liver. If the location of the liver in the etheric layers has shifted, the treatment might affect only the physical organ. In this case the treatment cannot achieve more than a partial and temporary success at best, because the pathogenic input from the etheric bodies continues to influence the liver detrimentally. If, however, all the etheric bodies are synchronized with the physical body, a faster, complete return to health may be expected.

Violet and the lighter shade of lavender link the body's energy fields with one another, and ensure that the etheric bodies are properly aligned. Sensitive individuals can, in fact, feel the movement as the fields realign when these cards are being used, and often find it exhausting.

Silver

In addition to the colours shown in Table 3, silver supplements the flower remedies red chestnut and cerato. It reflects negative or infringing energies back to their source, which helps strengthen people who tend to let themselves be dominated by others, individuals, for example, who are overly ready to enter into apparently symbiotic relationships (red chestnut), or are influenced beyond appropriate measure by the beliefs and opinions of others (cerato).

Pink

Pink enhances the effects of holly and its corresponding colour, blue. It should also be used with gorse, oak, pine, rock water, vine and willow, remedies for a lack of true love of self, which ultimately results in a lack of well-being and happiness.

6

EXPERIENCES WITH NATURAL HEALING

EVEN THOUGH we know quite a lot about the human organism and its biochemistry, the origins of many illnesses are still shrouded in mystery. The logic of science seems to require that every specific treatment should resolve the same specific problem every time, but this is not the case. Therapists of all medical orientations, orthodox and naturopathic, know that not every medication is equally good for everyone. There are, for example, antibiotics that can successfully eradicate bladder infections in a great many people while they fail to help others at all.

Similarly, some very reliable naturopathic methods of treatment sometimes fail to help particular individuals. I once assured a patient of mine that the pain in her knee would certainly be gone after a few acupuncture treatments, since I had never known this method to fail to relieve her kind of problem. She became my first failure, and to this day I do not know why her pain failed to respond to the treatment.

I have also had patients return to me after years of feeling well and say 'Please do again exactly what you did to me five years go; my migraines disappeared and have only just returned.' Despite giving them the identical treatment, success was much longer in coming than it had been the first time.

Of course, every therapist has probably also had the more pleasant, opposite experience: patients whom they had once tried to heal, suddenly respond immediately to the treatment that had failed earlier. One is simply left to wonder why it did not work the first time.

NOT EVERY AILMENT SHOULD BE 'CURED'

It is detrimental to a person to attempt to remove a symptom or problem that has a function in the body's whole system. The body's defences are then either so strongly directed against such intervention that the therapy fails, or the entire system is pushed to the brink of collapse.

I had a patient who had suffered from back pain because of a single dislocated vertebra; she wanted nothing more than to have this problem corrected. Numerous therapists before me had failed, and so did I. When dislocated vertebrae do not slip back into place easily, I prefer to leave them alone rather than to use force. Physiotherapy brings gradual relief for such ailments, and so I recommended a good physiotherapist to my patient. I did not know, however, that the physiotherapist had just completed a chiropractic course; he went to work putting the vertebra 'back where it belonged'. His success was accompanied by an audible crack. The patient was ecstatic – but only for an hour; then the pain returned more severely than before, and she developed a fever. When, after a week in bed, plagued by terrible pain, the woman recovered, it was found that her vertebra had slipped back into its old 'dislocated' position.

What had happened? The dislocation had an unknown but specific function in the woman's overall system, and removing the basis for this function resulted in a collapse. (This is often the case with precisely those patients who are most eager to have a condition cured.) I think that each human being is like a small universe, governed by its own specific laws and truths, created by the individual's consciousness and karmic links. Thus, the individual remains, in many ways, a mystery, perhaps even to him- or herself. The best that therapists can do is to learn from their experiences with all the different people they treat.

CRYSTAL ENERGY

My own experiences working with crystal energy have taught me many lessons. There are, for example, people who do not seem to respond to the colour normally successful in treating their ailment. In such cases it is always worth searching for the actual cause of their problems and working out an alternative approach. For example, if insomnia does not respond to the use of violet, it might be induced by an old habit or pattern, and in that case sky blue or indigo might be worth trying.

Some people are afraid to have their problems solved. I remember a young man who consulted me about his daily headaches. He told me that six years earlier he had had an acupuncture treatment that had eliminated his pain for three days. I asked him why he had not repeated the treatment. 'I don't know', he said simply. 'Even though I lived quite close to the practitioner, I never went back.' There is a difference between what we want consciously and what our subconscious demands. To gradually erode the discrepancy between the two, I suggest using sky blue, indigo and orange. The orange removes the fear of the new, unfamiliar situation in which the problem no longer has the significance we are used to attaching to it.

Sometimes illness can be a sort of self-punishment to compensate for feelings of guilt. Pink helps to open one up to the vibrations of love and self-esteem. It is enhanced by the flower remedies holly and pine.

The power of red

Low blood pressure responds to red and green. Slight or petite people who become cold easily usually need green to raise their blood pressure and to eliminate circulatory disorders, but may respond to the red crystal card with heart palpitations, shortness of breath or feeling of inner disquiet – all sure signs of intolerance. I have noticed that such people get a similar reaction if they wear jewellery with gemstones such as rubies, garnets or red tourmalines. Obviously, this is not the fault of the colour itself, but of the crystalline structure of the cards and gems, which enhances the power of the colour.

In her book about the healing properties of gemstones Hildegard of Bingen, the medieval naturopath, wrote that in the treatment of infections, shivering fits, fever and indigestion, for example, rubies should be placed on the patient's navel at midnight, but only long enough for the gems to warm up thoroughly to body temperature; they should then be removed at once, for longer contact would make them 'dry out' the body. 'Drying out' should probably be interpreted as meaning that the cardiovascular system is overstimulated by the red crystalline structure. Similarly, Chinese medicine maintains that over-stimulation of the heart produces an excess of 'fire', which harms the body by producing too much dryness, and can cause the psyche to become restless and rushed.

The influence of the moon

I have found that silver, a colour that reflects negative energies back to their source, is especially effective for people with round, chubby faces. Silver relates to the moon, and people who are strongly influenced by this heavenly body often have a so-called moon-face. A young woman of this description did not feel well at work. One of her co-workers was dabbling in magic, and had decided to test her abilities on this woman without the latter's knowledge. Finally, the young woman turned to the silver card for help, which, because of her own 'lunar' qualities, seems to have had a very powerful effect. The very first day she used it, her co-worker felt so uncomfortable that she asked to be moved to a different office.

Cats, dogs ... and batteries

Animals also respond well to treatment with crystal cards. For example, a cat that suffered from a persistently open wound on its forehead was given water that had been energized with the green card to drink. The injury was also washed with this water. After five days the sore, which had been open for months, had healed.

It is not unusual for dogs to become restless, to seem ill at ease anywhere in the house and constantly wander from room to room looking for a different place to sleep. Many dog owners have found that if they place a violet crystal card beneath a blanket, the dog will return to this place and quiet down there repeatedly.

A patient of mine found that crystal energy also affects non-living things. She told me that her watch had stopped and she needed a new battery. She put the watch in her jacket pocket, where it happened to lie against a gold crystal card. My patient forgot about the watch until she happened to wear that jacket again. Putting her hand into the pocket, she found the watch and noticed, to her great surprise, that it was running again. She expected that it would perhaps continue running for just a few days, but when she showed it to me, it had been running for three months, just as if she had put in a new battery.

This incident prompted the woman to experiment with other battery-powered devices. The batteries in her television remote-control had become quite weak, so she placed them on a green crystal card: after just one day, the control worked noticeably faster, and after a few days more, it worked like new. She also was able to eliminate static hissing, and variations in volume on her cordless telephone by placing it on a copper crystal card.

COLOUR YOURSELF
HEALTHY

Now that you have read about crystal and colour energies, I would like to encourage you to experiment and gain your own experiences. There is no shortage of opportunity for incorporating these beautiful colours in your daily life. Sometimes it is enough merely to absorb a colour that appeals to you at a particular moment. This is a method commonly used in kinesiology to relieve stress and you might find it a useful place to begin.

Collect ten to twelve different colours of tissue paper or glossy paper, and cut out postcard-size pieces. If there is no one to help you, spread the samples out in front of you and keep looking at them until you are drawn to one colour. If you have a partner to help you, use the kinesiology test explained earlier in 'Some Practical Applications of Crystal Cards'; when your arm can resist your partner's pressure, you have found the right colour for you.

After you have found the correct colour, visualize coating your entire body with it, inside and out. Close your eyes and begin colouring yourself internally. You will notice that some parts of your body seem almost to colour themselves, while others absorb the colour only with a lot of effort. Take your time, and meditate yourself into the colour. When you think you are finished, inspect yourself with your inner eye, checking every nook and cranny. Is every part of you evenly coated? If so, begin colouring yourself on the outside in the same way. Work systematically, starting at your feet and moving upwards until you have 'dyed' your hair.

Are you now completely saturated with your colour? Did you take enough time to cope with stubborn spots? If so, you can sit back and enjoy the sense of having all the pores and tissues of your body soaking up the colour you need, and drawing on its strength for regeneration and calming. Try to maintain this visualization for as long as you can, and enjoy it! Even when you are short of time, spend at least five to ten minutes on this exercise.

Despite the clear and obvious effects that colours and crystalline structures have on our well-being, if you suffer from serious or persistent health problems, you should, of course, consult a doctor or other health-care professional.

But you are quite free at all times to support and enhance any prescription treatment with other, gentler energies. Health problems are usually not due to a single cause, and respond to many different approaches. Sensible health-care practitioners will not object to your using other, supportive methods that do not interfere with their treatment.

APPENDIX

INDEX OF CRYSTAL CARD APPLICATIONS

This index will enable you to choose the correct colour for specific conditions and ailments. The list is in alphabetical order by symptom or problem, and, where necessary, instructions for where to apply the card and for how long are given.

When you carry crystal cards with you, the negative side usually faces the body. You can experiment with the positioning of the cards, and you can repeat the application until you have achieved the desired result. However, for therapeutic uses, the cards should not be in direct contact with the body for more than twenty minutes.

To energize liquids, place them on the appropriate card for thirty minutes. Sip the liquid three times a day. I suggest placing a glass bottle with your drinking and plant water on the green card. This way the water is continuously energized and you can simply refill the bottle without watching the time exactly; normally it takes twenty to thirty minutes to energize a bottle of water.

Once a week cleanse each card by holding it under cold running water. The black card should be cleansed like this more frequently because it absorbs negative energies like a sponge.

Problem	Colour	Instructions
Acne	Green	Place card on affected area; drink energized water; wash affected area with energized water
Alcoholism	Violet	Carry card with you
Allergies, general	Violet	Carry card with you
Allergies, food	Violet	Place foods on card
Arthritis	Red, green, orange	Place one card on each side of the affected area, and carry red with you
Asthma	Gold, indigo	Place gold on the left lung, indigo over the right, and switch after ten minutes
Athlete's foot	Orange	Place card in shoe for two days
Athletic performance	Red	Carry card with you
Back pain	Violet	Sleep on card
Bed-wetting	Violet	Place card under pillow at night
Bladder, weakness of	Red	Place card on bladder area
Bleeding	Blue	Place on affected area
Blood pressure, high	Blue, green	Place one card on either side of chest, switch after ten minutes

Problem	Colour	Instructions
Bone deterioration	Red, green, orange	Place red on affected area, drink water energized with orange and green
Brain hemispheres unbalanced	Violet	Wear one card on each side of the head, tucked under a headband
Bronchitis	Yellow	Place card for ten minutes on both lungs and then, for another ten minutes, on upper chest towards armpits
Bruises	Green	Place on the affected area
Burns	Blue	Place on affected area
Care-givers, supporting combination for	Gold, silver	Before and after treating patients, place gold under right foot and silver under left foot
Circulation, poor	Red	Carry card with you
Colds	Blue, yellow	Place one card on each lung, and switch after ten minutes
Concentration, poor	Yellow	Carry card with you
Constipation	Yellow	Place card on lower abdomen
Cough	Red	Place card on throat or chest
Deafness	Gold, red, green	Place gold on top and a little towards the back of the head; place red and green on the ears, positive sides touching the skin, and switch after ten minutes

78

Problem	Colour	Instructions
Depression	Violet, black	Carry both cards with you
Diarrhoea	Turquoise	Place card on abdomen, and drink energized water
Digestion, disturbances of	Orange	Place card on stomach
Digestion, weakness of	Gold, indigo	Place both cards on stomach for ten minutes, positives sides facing the body
Disquiet, restlessness	Violet	Carry card with you
Dreams, to remember	Gold, violet	Place both cards beneath pillow
Drug addiction	Violet	Carry card with you
Earache	Lime green	Place card on ears
Ear blockages	Yellow	Place card on ears
Emotional instability	Lavender	Place card on forehead
Epilepsy	Blue	Carry card with you
Exhaustion	Turquoise, blue	Carry cards with you
Eyesight, weakness of	Turquoise	Place card on eyes for ten minutes
Fatigue	Red	Drink energized water
Feet, cold	Copper	Put a card into each shoe; if you put a card into only one shoe, the other foot will remain cold

Problem	Colour	Instructions
Feet, sore	Violet	Place cards in shoes
Fever	Yellow	Drink energized water; place card on nape of neck and then on forehead, with positive side touching the body
Fungus	Indigo, yellow	Wash affected areas with energized water
Hair loss	Gold	Sleep with one card on either side of the head for three months; put a tourmaline in the shampoo
Headache	Violet	Place card on head or forehead
Healing	Lavender, violet, red	Place lavender beside patient, violet on top of and a little towards the back of the head, and red on pubic bone
Heartburn	Green	Place card on stomach
Haemorrhoids	Green	Place card on affected area, and wash with energized water
Hormone imbalance	Blue	Carry card with you
Hyperkinetics	Blue, indigo, violet	Before going to bed, drink water energized with blue; place indigo card under foods, and energize daily drinking water with violet
Infections	Indigo, yellow, green	Place indigo and yellow or green cards on the affected areas
Insect stings and bites	Violet	Place card on affected area

Problem	Colour	Instructions
Insomnia	Violet	Place card under pillow
Itching	Blue	Place card on affected area
Kidney trouble	Green	Drink energized water
Labour pains	Violet, blue	Hold one card in each hand for ten minutes, then switch
Learning disability	Violet, yellow	Carry cards with you
Ligaments, pulled	Blue, green	Apply cards crosswise over affected area
Menstrual cramps	Green	Place card on stomach
Migraine headache	Violet, black	Apply violet vertically and black horizontally on top, on affected area
Muscle aches	Orange	Place card on affected area; use energized massage oil
Muscle, pulled	Violet, green, blue	Apply violet card first to soothe pain, then bandage area with green card on one side and blue on the other
Nappy rash	Violet	Place nappies on card before use; place card briefly on skin
Negative energy	Black, gold	Carry both cards with you
Nervousness	Violet	Carry card with you
Pain, general	Violet	Place card on affected area
Pains, phantom	Lavender	Carry card with you, as close to the body as possible

Problem	Colour	Instructions
Parasites	Yellow	Wash with energized water
Planets, retrograde	Violet	Carry card with you
Plants, sickly	Green	Water plants with energized water
Premenstrual tension (PMT)	Green	Carry card with you
Psoriasis	Violet, green	Carry violet card with you; drink water energized with green and use it to wash affected areas
Puberty	Blue, indigo, violet	Carry cards with you; absolutely do not use red
Radiation exposure	Black, gold	Carry both cards with you during exposure, such as when working at a computer
Radiation in food	Black	Place foods on card
Rash	Violet	Carry card with you
Self-esteem, lack of	Pink	Carry card with you
Seasickness	Turquoise	Carry card with you
Sexual drive too strong	Turquoise	Place on sexual organs
Sexual drive too weak	Red	Place on sexual organs

Problem	Colour	Instructions
Sinus congestion	Violet, red, blue	Carry violet with you; place red and blue on sinuses, and switch them after ten minutes
Smoking, to stop	Indigo, gold	Carry cards with you
Sore throat	Blue	Place card on throat
Sores, open	Green	Drink energized water, and use it to wash sores
Splinters	Green	Place on inflamed area
Stomach discomfort	Orange	Place card on stomach
Stress	Violet, blue	Carry violet with you; drink water energized with blue
Stuttering	Dark blue, sky blue	Carry cards with you
Sunburn	Blue	Place card on affected area
Sunburn, protection against	Lavender, black	Carry cards with you
Teething	Violet	Hold card on affected area
Thyroid, overactive	Indigo	Place card on thyroid gland
Thyroid, underactive	Blue	Place card on thyroid gland
Toothache	Violet	Place card on affected area

Problem	Colour	Instructions
Toxicity in body	Green	Drink energized water
Travel sickness	Turquoise	Carry card with you
Underweight	Blue	Carry card with you
Vomiting	Indigo	Carry card with you
Water retention	Violet	Carry card with you
Warts	Lime green	Place card on affected area
Whiplash injury	Black, sky blue	Carry black with you and place on affected area; carry sky blue with you for about an hour at first, and increase time gradually
Wrinkles	Violet	Place card under pillow
Yin and yang, to balance	Gold, silver	Place gold card under right foot, and silver under left

ASTROLOGICAL SIGNS AND CRYSTAL COLOURS

Aries	Red
Taurus	Blue and black
Gemini	Violet
Cancer	Green
Leo	Orange
Virgo	Turquoise
Libra	Yellow
Scorpio	Red
Sagittarius	Lime green
Capricorn	Blue
Aquarius	Green and blue
Pisces	Indigo

RESOURCES

Crystal cards are available in credit card format or as small equilateral triangles. Both have the same effects. The triangles, also known as Rainbow Charms, are pierced in one corner and come with a jump ring so that they can be worn as jewellery.

MANUFACTURER

Micro-Crystal Corporation
P.O. Box 166
Greenville, Michigan 48838
USA

SUPPLIERS

Colour Institute of Canada
P.O. Box 59
Perkinsfield, Ontario LOL 2J0
Canada

Arcania
17 Union Passage
Bath
Avon BA1 1RS
England

Gothic Image Ltd
7 High Street
Glastonbury
Somerset BA6 9DP
England

INDEX

For treatment of individual problems, refer also to the Index of Crystal Card Applications on p.76.